The 11 Forgotten Laws

Success Elements

By Monica Selph

"The mind is its own place, and in itself, can make heaven of Hell and a hell of Heaven."
- John Milton

Disclaimer

Contents

The Forgotten Laws

The "Forgotten" Laws have been debated over for many, many years, and eventually, there is no doubt that these laws are universal and applicable to all human beings.

So why does it happen that some people find them to be successful and useful, while others receive no success from them?

The truth is, there is much more than meets the eye when it comes to the forgotten laws. People might read them thoroughly and try to figure out what they are and how they can be implemented in their own lives.

However, what they fail to realize is that in order to make these laws work to your advantage, it isn't important to know what the laws are initially, but more important to know who YOU are. Then only can these forgotten laws be used to your advantage.

It is not an easy task to tap into your inner self and to find out who you are, but until and unless you do, the forgotten laws will be of no benefit to you. They ask that you dig deep down into yourself and push out the power within you. The forgotten laws will give you everything you need, from self-confidence, to learning how to forgive people.

They touch upon all aspects of your life to ensure that you change your life for the better. By understanding the forgotten laws you will realize how much potential is within you.

If you look at your life right now, without the forgotten laws, you can compare yourself to Pinocchio the puppet. He was made of wood and controlled by strings. But, he had the will to be a boy. This is where the forgotten laws come into play. Pinocchio wanted to be a boy so badly that he became real.

The forgotten laws work in this way. If you want something badly, you can get it, by putting in all the energy and strength you possess within yourself.

Law of Thinking

The proverb, "As a man thinketh in his heart, so is he," best describes the foundation of a human being's life. It really reflects deeply on the fact that most human beings really end up becoming who they think they want to eventually become.

Numerous leaders across the world, whether they are heads of state, business tycoons, or even at the managerial level all agreed with this proverb unanimously.

Why did they agree to it without thinking about it twice?

This is because they imagined and pictured themselves being in a position of power far before they actually realized their dreams. This shows how important the Law of Thinking is in attaining success.

We have to learn how to break the shackles of what society expects us to be and how certain expectations they have from us. Expectations only limit successful people because dreamers dream far beyond just meeting other peoples' expectations.

Dreamers at some point in their lives learn how to take full control over their lives and steer their own ship to their desired destination.

Humans have a natural tendency to think that certain factors are beyond our control. But if you really sit down and think about it, every factor is in our control, it just depends on how we choose to react to it and how well prepared we are.

It is common for people to blame the government or the economy for not being a comfortable position after the recession, but what about those whose business have shown double digit growth in the same period when others were going bankrupt?

This all has to do with the Law of Thinking and how we can use it to our advantage by being prepared and accepting for change.

In this Law, we learn how to access infinite possibilities even from worst-case scenarios and turn them into brilliant ideas.

Being unable to easily find solutions to problems such as becoming financially free, there is a discontent and dissatisfaction that sparks within us.

Over time, that spark becomes into a raging fire of discontent, which makes us think "outside the box" and we implement ideas that very few before have even thought of. This is the beauty of the Law of Thinking. We have to learn how to directly communicate with our mind and guide it towards success. Once the idea forms in our mind, then it gives rise to actions which we take to improve our lives.

But these ideas don't just sprout up whenever you feel like having them. Most humans believe life to be a mystery, in which there is a lot that is unexplained and impenetrable. But in reality it is quite simple because mystery is often linked to ignorance.

Once we learn how to start "knowing" exactly what we want, then there remains no mystery, hence, no ignorance.

Our mind is like a blossoming flower, it needs the adequate amount of water and sunlight to flourish and dazzle the world with its beauty one day.

Just like that flower never ceases to stop growing as long as it is provided sunlight and water, our mind never stops pushing itself further as long we keep pushing it further.

The Law of Thinking clearly states that we need to focus and concentrate hard on thoughts which we want to materialize.

It is also notice people on a daily basis, they the thoughts they predominantly and most commonly think of, manifest into their everyday lives.

However, the problem lies in us thinking about all the WRONG things.

The truth of the matter is that if most people are asked to speak their minds, they would not even have a word to say.

How can we expect our mind to accomplish great feats and help us become successful if we don't channel the right energy it?

That is why we need to constantly focus and pinpoint thoughts in our mind to make them materialize one day.

Now most people here might say, "Everyone has the capability to think, so of course they think!" This is far from the truth, just because we are initiating mental processes within our mind, doesn't mean that we are thinking.

Thinking involved analyses from various perspectives, deduction, induction, and most importantly, intellect.

We confuse mental activity as thinking because our five senses are always presenting new information to our brain.

Whether it's the color of the dress an attractive woman is wearing or the smell of freshly grilled barbeque, our senses are always bombarding our brain with information. Therefore, it becomes difficult for our conscious part of the brain to retain every single piece of information.

We have to step in and become progressive beings by filtering information that is not as important because the growth of the brain is directly correlated to the amount of intellectual thinking we do daily.

Most people are so bogged down in their regular routines that they fail to break the cycle and help their mind grow.

Whether it's the 9 to 5 job where employees toil away or watching TV endlessly in the evening, these actions do not help your mind progress.

What our mind needs is a challenge waiting around every corner. And as it overcomes each obstacle, it begins to really gain momentum like a snowball down a steep hill.

By the end, our mind is so receptive and so aware of pertinent information, there is no stopping it on the way to success.

You need to break the monotony and direct all the forces into constructive channels for constant progression and advancement. If you begin to think upward bound starting tomorrow, you can notice the positive influence it brings upon your life.

On the other hand, if your mind is downward bound, you will always feel like you're stuck in a place of discord, discontentment, and disappointment. These negative feelings will then guide your mind the wrong way, away from success.

So you might ask, "How do I make my mind go upward bound?" The primary step is to strongly believe in what you want. If there is no belief, there will never be a materialization or

Walk By Faith (Belief)
Not By Sight (Circumstance)

11

realization of the belief. It is best to do what you want to do, rather than what you "think" you can do.

The majority of humans are discouraged from doing what they really WANT to do and instead, they are encouraged to do what they "should" do.

This is where the shackles have to break and you have to let loose to find freedom.

Freedom to think on an intellectual level and the freedom to do exactly what you want with full conviction.

Law of Supply

This quote from the New Testament best describes the Law of Supply. People in the modern age assume that we should always be satisfied with what we have and with what has been given to us.

To a certain extent, this is applicable because as humans, we should always be grateful and thankful for what we have, but never satisfied. The day we become satisfied with what we have, that is the day we stop trying to push our success further.

Just as the New Testament describes, we should always be searching for new ways to succeed and if we keep trying, one of the doors will be opened to us and result in financial freedom.

The only thing that can stop us from achieving our goals, is sheer ignorance.

The only way to eliminate ignorance is through learning. How did we move past the ignorance of accepting slavery?

How did we move past the ignorance smoking indoors with other non-smokers present?

When we are learning, we have to get an understanding of what the matter at hand is.

The Law of Supply indicates that there is plenty for us to strive for out there. We should never sit satisfied in a corner thinking that there isn't enough for us.

However, when we are stuck under the wrong impression that there is nothing out there for us, it is simply ignorance and us trying to see things through a blindfold.

Once you are able to remove that blindfold, you can clearly see that there are plenty of opportunities waiting to be capitalized on by us.

Others might keep on telling you how bleak the outlook may appear, but you have to break through this layer of negativity and come out a new person on top.

When Thomas Edison invented the first light bulb, believe it or not, most people were apprehensive about it because some thought it was unsafe while others thought it consumed too much electricity. So they stuck closely to their candles, which in reality were nowhere near as effective as a light bulb.

What this story indicates is that the masses are resistant to change. In the majority of cases, change occurs for the better, not for the worse.

Yet human psyche is conditioned to think that change is a bad thing, therefore, we must do every conceivable thing to prevent the change from coming about.

But those who are willing to adapt and transform, are the ones who can reach the pinnacle of success.

Those who dare to dream and realize the potential of the law of supply are able to manifest their inner most goals and live a life of unbridled success.

The Law of Supply also works in another very interesting way. If you break your shell and step out of your comfort zone to take the bull by its horns, people will respect you and appreciate you for who you are.

If we are talking about this aspect of the Law in corporate terms, if there is a creation of a need and then eventually a solution or answer to that need, the demand will follow.

Similarly, as stated previously, there is always supply because there will always be demand.

Your share of the pie depends on how hungry you are to go and get it. Another prime example is of the Wright Brothers who invented the first airplane.

In that day and age, no one in their right mind thought that they would sit on a flying aircraft that would take them thousands of feet above the ground and move them from one place to another.

People were too apprehensive about the safety, logistics, and several other factors regarding aerial flight. These weren't dreamers, they were just by standers watching greatness unravel before their very own eyes. Yet, they still initially failed to realize the greatness of the idea until others chimed in and decided that the airplane was a revolutionary invention.

Thanks to the Wright Brothers who were dreamers, they managed to step out to the corner of the ledge and take a chance with their ideas.

They realized that the demand in the long run would be a never-ending opportunity and they were certainly on the mark. They created the primary method of transportation used in the modern world for far-away destinations.

Law of Attraction

Another law of the universe is the law of attraction. The law of attraction is the idea that by outputting positive energy into the world, and thinking positively will bring about positive things and outcomes.

When you have negative thoughts and energy, then negative things will happen to you.

The law of attraction is a law that has a base within this universe. Natural laws are laws that cannot be changed or altered.

They connect human beings as well as all things on this planet. Now with the law of attraction, you can decide on what your future will hold and how it will unfold through the power of the mind.

How? If you read through this section, you'll find out how you can master the law of attraction and can make your life exactly what you want it to be.

The law of attraction pulls you towards or pulls you away from everything on this earth which can feel, draw and repel energy. What your subconscious energy needs it will be drawn to. The way you perceive life and how you live is a complete reflection of what your naturally are drawn to and what you naturally want and feel about certain wants and needs.

For example, if you want to make more money and to become more financially stable, you can focus all your thoughts and energy towards this want.

By focusing positive energy towards your goal will allow the environment around you to become conducive to your goal and will help you achieve your goal.

Now if this concept is a little hard to grasp, let's discuss it in terms of energy. Energy is the force that can do something or change something.

The earth is made up of various energies working in cohesion. Through this energy everyone and everything is connected.

Through the cohesive movement, certain energies are attracted to other energies and others are repelled. You as a human being possess an energy and can interact with other energies through yourself.

Through your energy you can change circumstances and outcomes of your life.

The path you choose with the positive or negative energy you posses will allow you to have the life you want to lead and will help you avoid the life you do not want to live.

Through motivation, passion, and determination, your energy can help you achieve things you've only dreamt of. With a power like this, there is no stopping you!

The law of attraction has been a law since the inception of the earth and all other universal laws.

While it may have taken time for some people to understand that power of attraction, one of the first men to embrace this power was Buddha. Buddha embraced the ideology of the law of attraction and tried to spread this power onto his disciples.

Buddha's main principle was the idea that a human being had particular characteristics because that human being thought of those characteristics continuously. The way Buddha summed it up was, "What you have become is what you have thought."

By embracing thought and power, people were able to get in tune with themselves, their environments, and nature and were able to choose the path they wanted their life to proceed on.

Starting in the East, the law of attraction took on different forms among different cultures. The idea of karma may have arisen from this ideology.

Karma is basically the concept that if you are good to others, good things will happen to you, and if you are bad to others, that negativity will come back to haunt you one day. Through your actions and interactions you can change energy and can have some grasp on the energy that comes back to you.

The law of attraction came over to North America in the 1800s and was spread through the efforts of William Walker Atkinson. Atkinson led the way to the New Thought movement in the United States by writing over 100 publications on the subject.

The New Thought movement was the ideal that your spirit is the highest power and that through your own self you could harness the divine power you posses inside you to help keep away physical illnesses and use the power of the mind to heal yourself.

The ideal that a higher power exists is there, but in the form of spirit and energy within each and every human being.

The law of attraction has been around for decades and has been enlightening a certain few over the years, allowing them to control their destinies.

Emitting positive or negative energy can change your life and future, so understanding how to grasp the ideology of the law of attraction and using it to your benefit will only improve your life and the life of those around you.

By outputting positive energy into the world, you are helping positive energy circulate around your environment and other people, making the world a better place to live in for yourself, your family, and your future generations.

Now when it comes to applying the law of attraction, you'll need to know how to use it so that you can benefit from it.

When you fully understand the law of attraction and know how to use it, you will be able to change every aspect of your life.

The first thing you will want to do is accept every event that has happened in your life, whether positive or negative. You need to come to terms with everything that has happened by understanding that you were the one controlling the outcome of the event.

Usually we are taught that our environment impacts the outcome of the events in our lives, but in reality, through the law of attraction, we control the environment as well as the outcome of the events that occur in our lives.

Write down each event and take a few minutes to reflect on how it made you feel.

What you will find is a common trend of a string of positive and negative energy at specific times in life. While good events happened in life, you'll realize how you had felt and felt after the event took place. The same goes with

21

negative events. At the times that negative outcomes occurred, you'll find that you were in a dark place or were thinking negative thoughts at the time.

Secondly you'll want to understand the fact that you are in control of your destiny and your environment. You alone can control what happens depending on how you think about it and how you feel.

Decide on what aspects of your life you want to change and how you want to change it. By embracing the power that you have over your life, you are allowing yourself to benefit fully from the law of attraction.

Write all your goals down and put them on your fridge, on your phone, on your computer, etc. Basically you'll want to put them in plain sight so you can constantly think about them and strive to reach the goals.

When these thoughts are consistently in your head, the energy you emit will be drawn to the energy that can help you achieve these goals.

You will be more attracted to the path that leads to your goals and which will allow you to reach your goals easily and quickly.

Next you'll want to start thinking positively and emitting positive vibes. When you are happy and positive, your energy will be drawn to positive and happy energies in the universe.

When your attitude is positive, your actions will be positive. If you may encounter obstacles on the way to reaching your goals, staying positive will help you overcome those obstacles.

Channeling your energy to positive actions can help you reach your goals faster.

Lastly, always have faith in yourself. When you believe you can do anything and achieve everything you want to, you will feel the energy that is within you.

Everybody has insecurities and doubts, but pushing past those doubts and insecurities strengthens you as an individual and helps you push towards your goal. When you believe in yourself, nobody and nothing can deter you from your goals.

The power within you can be harnessed and can help you change the world you live in.

When you follow each and every one of these steps, you will see your lives will change. You will be able to set a goal for yourself, believe in it entirely, and then to channel all your energy into achieving those goals.

When you finally reach those goals, you will realize the power you have within yourself and that power cannot be deterred by anything or anyone. So give yourself the chance to try and harness your energy to get everything you want and deserve.

Law of Receiving

The law of receiving is a law that helps you understand the concept of giving and receiving.

Receiving is a concept that is not just about yourself, but also about the person giving you something. It is a two-side story in which you need to realize and fully identify with both perspectives to really appreciate your position.

Without grasping both positions of giving and receiving, you cannot fully value the actions. The two actions are inseparable and when you accept both actions, you will accept the law of receiving.

The three things you will need to learn about before accepting the gift of receiving have to do with understanding your position in life and pushing for more.

First, to understand what receiving is, you have to give. When you give, you really start to appreciate the feeling that comes with giving. The action of giving is a powerful action and is the catalyst to the law of receiving.

The ultimate concept is that when you give, you will receive, and the more you give, the more you will receive. That is the ideology you want to understand and believe in.

Embodying this concept will help you be drawn to the things that you can receive. You will be drawn to the things you deserve by giving to others and the environment.

To understand the importance of giving, you need to help yourself by giving back for the things you receive.

The second concept in the law of receiving that you'll want to understand is how to receive and how to ready yourself to receive.

When you give, then you should expect to receive. If you believe in the first step, that the more you give, the more you receive, then you'll understand how important this step is.

Just as in science, to every action there is a reaction, however, it may not be an equal and opposite reaction.

If you receive something after giving, and it is exactly what you wanted, then the law of receiving is on the right path.

However, it does happen at times that you do not receive what you wanted, therefore, you look back at the first step and see what you've done wrong.

When you fully embody and think about receiving everything you want and need, your body and energy will be drawn to success.

Your energy will automatically be drawn to successful and positive energy, changing your environment, allowing yourself to receive everything you deserve to go down the path of success.

If you do not get what you want, and are confused as to why you haven't had your expected results, you'll want to know that your mind needs to be completely clear and focused.

You need to open yourself to the idea behind the law of receiving and understand the value of it.

Realizing the full value of life changing actions can take time to understand and can be overwhelming, but if you prepare yourself, then you'll know that you're at the next stage of the law of receiving.

When you've understood the concept behind giving, and have prepared yourself to receive, you then need to understand that what you want will never be too much for you to receive or achieve.

The more you push yourself to receive, the more you will receive. If you want a little, then you will receive only a little, but if you want more, and understand that your wants are limitless, you are opening yourself up to a new lifestyle and a new attitude.

The more you give of yourself and to others, the more you will receive. If you wholeheartedly give and want to receive, you will receive that exact same amount.

Putting your entire body, mind and soul into the things you want will get you want you want, and only through the power of belief in yourself and your natural abilities.

When you read through the law of receiving and completely understand it, you'll realize that it encompasses all different laws. It pushes you to understand that without embodying the law of supply, the law of attraction, the law of thinking, etc., you will not be able to get the things you want and need.

Understanding these laws, and understanding the value of what you have within yourself will help you get the things you need and will help you change your outlook on life.

These life changing laws will help you change your attitude and will open you up to the positive things the world has to offer and the positive things you have to offer the world.

Everybody has a particular amount of energy, but those who choose to emit that energy and understand it are more successful because they understand the power they have in themselves.

To understand what you have inside you, you need to be open to everything that can help you get there. It is as if you are a magnet, pulling in all positive forces to help you push your positive energy out in a more conducive environment.

Opening yourself up to a positive environment can be scary and can sometimes bring on the unexpected. This is part of receiving. You need to take things as they come and look at them in a positive attitude.

When you change your attitude, your environment will change, and you will understand how through the power you possess you can change your future and destiny.

Opening yourself up to good things will only bring on better things more consistently. It is about understanding the value of yourself and the life around you.

Positive energy attracts positive energy, and when you full understand that concept, you will be living it.

The universe is a strong and full of energy, so letting yourself be part of the energy and feeding off of it and allowing it to feed off of you will only get you the things you deserve.

Law of Increase

The law of increase is one of the Forgotten Laws that will help change your life when you start to understand its power.

Every forgotten law is interlinked to each other and to grasp each one to its full extent is vital to understand its power. So what is the law of increase?

It is the law of wanting to do better and increasing productivity, success, and positivity in your life.

For example, if someone tells you you've done a good job, what do you feel? Not only do you feel good, you feel like you want to continue doing a good job as well as maybe push yourself harder to do even better.

The positive reinforcement helps you increase your goals. This is what the law of increase is about.

When given a compliment, you feel good about yourself. You feel grateful for the good positive comments and it is an added boost to your ego. It feels good to be complimented and has a variety of positive effects on your body and mind.

When you understand that you are emitting goodness and positive energy into the world, you'll receive more positive and good energy back, which can change your life. More often than not, people always focus on the things that are lacking in their life or the negative things that happen to them.

This closes you off to positive energy and closes you off to receiving the good in the world. With more negative thought comes more negative energy, therefore, the law of increase teaches you and pushes you to do more positive things so you have more positive things happen to you in your life. It is almost like the saying, "what you give is what you get".

Did your mother ever scold you if you said something mean to a sibling or cousin? She'd say, "Treat people like you would want to be treated yourself."

This advice is not only good to teach children, but it is actually very powerful, especially when you start to understand the power of the mind.

The power of goodness attracts other goodness in the world, therefore, will help you open yourself up to goodness and success the world can offer you.

Now, when trying to increase, you'll need to focus on what you want to increase and how. Having a clear focus on what you want in life is extremely important. You could want a number of things that you'd want to "increase" in your life, be it money, health, relationships, etc.

The way you perceive these things and the way you go about getting them is extremely important. It cannot be stressed how important positive energy is and how to emit it.

For instance, if you want to have more money, you'll want to go about it by focusing on it and working towards it physically and mentally.

While on the road to more success, you may come across people who may have more money than you.

Although your first reaction may be jealousy, you should control yourself. There is no reason to be jealous of someone if they have more money than you.

The truth is that this person who may have more money than you may have it because of hard work and focus, something that should be appreciated and admired.

Feeling envious is a negative energy which will only attract negative energy towards you. Feeling hatred or negative feelings towards people will not help you in any way, therefore, it's important to continue staying happy for those around you and to push yourself to reach your goal.

If the law of increase is a little confusing to understand, you may want to look at it like this. Whatever you give time and effort to, it will increase. For example, if you start a new relationship, you'll need to put time and effort into it to ensure that it will be a good relationship and that it will last forever. The more effort put into the relationship, the better it will be. This ideology works in all aspects of your life.

For instance, if you start a new business, you'll need to put your own money into it and will obviously have to work hard to get it off the ground and full functioning.

The more money and hard work you put into the business, the more money you will make. Now, there are times when you can invest in things that won't give you a profit, but the act of putting more money into your business will not hurt it in any way, your profits will eventually increase if you continue working hard on it.

Working towards something won't ever hurt you, even if you don't get the expected outcome. Working towards something and learning how to give will make the act of receiving more meaningful and valuable.

Focus is very important when trying to reach your goals, and obstacles are part of the process. Pushing past the obstacles and pushing to get to your goal is what the law of increase stresses. Pushing past the things that may obstruct your path to your goals will help you understand the importance of giving more to getting more. The more you invest in yourself, the more you will get for yourself.

Law of Compensation

The law of Compensation is one of the most vital yet basic laws of life and is often referred to as "the great law." Ancient civilizations were also aware of this law and they knew it as "Karma."

This law has a scientific basis and it is parallel to the law of action and reaction as well as the law of cause and effect. Just as we know there is a reaction to ever action, similarly, the law of compensation indicates to us that our actions have certain repercussions.

Although the reactions of our actions may not come forth in the immediate future, they will come about at some point in our lives.

Karma teaches us the fact that there are consequences in life regarding the steps we take. Often, success is right in front of us, yet the journey we have to take towards it is underhanded and not right.

Most people would think that success is success, therefore, it does not matter how you get there as long as you do. This however is a fallacy because it is the journey that is more important than the destination.

It is the struggle and hard work we put in the journey of reaching our end goal which makes us heroes capable of praise. The law of compensation is not something that should only be temporarily followed, instead it is an ideology that should become a way of life.

By taking control, we can start believing that our destiny is in our control. We can become go-getters instead of passively watch the world go by.

Karma teaches us the responsibility of taking the right actions, actions that do not bring harm unto other people and actions that are taken with the right intentions.

When it comes to the law of compensation, the most positive reactions come from the purest motives.

Jesus discussed the law of compensation indirectly by explaining it as the principle of sowing and reaping, giving and receiving, and doing unto others as you would have them do unto you.

He understood and propagated the law of compensation because of the benefits it provided to those who followed it. Just as there is a cycle of life, there is a cycle of action and reaction.

Neither can it ever be stopped or delayed, for when the time comes for a reaction of an action to take place, it is going to occur. What we can ensure is that the reaction is a positive one and this can be done be taking positive, selfless, and mutually beneficial actions.

There are some people out there who do not believe in the existence of such a law because the end result or reaction may take years or even decades to produce itself and appear.

Therefore human understanding might forgo the chance to take opportunity from the law of compensation.

Several people also believe that our actions might not have reactions in this lifetime at all, and that it is in the next life which will show us the consequences of all our negative or positive reactions.

Regardless of when and how you think the reactions will come, it is essential to know that they WILL come one day, whether you like it or not.

So if you have been carrying out positive and selfless actions throughout your life, you will have nothing to fear and can only expect the best in return.

However, if you have not taken the "correct" and "virtuous" decisions in order to reach your end goal, then you might not like what is in store for you.

It is never too late to change things around and start doing them the right way.

We all have inherent goodness in us and through the use of the law of compensation, we can spread goodness and cheer all over and even expect it in return. At some point, good things will start happening with you as a reciprocation of the noble actions you took before.

A very simple yet moving story clearly illustrates the benefits of positive actions in our lives.

There was a couple that used to work as servants in a household. They would perform such duties as cooking, cleaning, and various other activities.

They came from very humble beginnings and had never experienced the luxuries of life that their employers could afford.

However, this did not matter to them because they believed in doing their chores and not being jealous of anyone.

They went about their life happily, and were able to have one child in their lifetime. They raised the boy to be an upstanding citizen, and led by example.

The mother, father, and boy were all treated well in the house they worked at, like members of the house, because the owner of the house always had a soft spot for them in his heart.

He knew he could not find people as honest and reliable as this family.

So he constantly tried to give them anything they desired, yet, they never desired anything more than their monthly wages, food, and a place to sleep.

The only son observed how his parents lived and at times he used to get frustrated about why they were so content even though there were so many extravagances that they were missing out on.

One day the father saw the anguish on his son's face and sat him down. The father said, "Son, there is an equal and opposite reaction to every action we take in life.

Depending on how inherently good that action is, we are either punished or rewarded by the reaction we get in return." The boy looked on confusingly as his father further explained.

"We should always take the virtuous path to reach our goals and avoid taking shortcuts just to say that yes, we achieved our goals.

Goals are worthless if the path taken to reach those goals is malicious or improper. Therefore, we as good human beings should always focus on bringing happiness and contentment to others."

All this talk seemed quite ideological and the boy was not fully convinced due to his immaturity and impatience. As life went on, the owner of the house, who had three children, began to fall ill more often as he aged.

The owner's children were not very sympathetic to their father, and were not prime examples of how loving and caring children should be.

They would call a few times a year from their faraway places of residence, namely on the big holidays such as Christmas or Thanksgiving.

Yet, they rarely found time to visit their old ailing father who just needed some love and affection, especially in his last days of existence.

The owner of the house was always an upright being who believed in working hard with complete honesty. This is why he at times treated the help in his house more like his own family.

His children were obviously not too ecstatic about this fact and further chose to ignore their father and not give him any time of day.

In reality, the owner did not need them, because he had the ultimate care giving family already in his house. He had a family that was his support system when he was down, a family that shared their happiness and sorrow with him and vice versa, and a family that would do anything to bring joy to the now old and fragile man.

One day the owner felt more down than usual and quickly realized that today was going to be his last day.

He called the help to come around his bedside, where they all stood with tears in their eyes, watching their dependable and extremely caring role model slowly drift away into oblivion.

As the owner of the house spoke incoherently, he pointed his finger towards an envelope with the family's name on it. The young boy looked on curiously as to what was in the envelope.

Paying no attention to what was in it, the mother and father came close to their master's bedside, holding his hand and sobbing. After some time, they realized that the warmth in their master's hands had faded and that the time they dreaded the most had come.

After serving the owner of the house for over three decades, the helping family did not know how to go on with life without the presence and assistance of the old man.

Heartbroken, the father of the family took the envelope in his hands, hesitating to open it, and not feeling comfortable to read it without the owner's children's permission.

Yet, he could clearly see that his name was written on the envelope, so after some contemplation, he opened the envelope.

In the envelope was a letter, written by the owner of the house for the father, mother, and son. The letter was a will that the old man had left behind. From what it appeared, the master never lived his life extravagantly, so it never seemed like he had much wealth. However, it turned out that he owned land which contained oil thousands of miles underground. This land was worth millions if not billions of dollars, and all of the money was left behind to the family.

The moral of this story clearly is that if you put in hard work with diligence and ignore whatever luxuries you may be missing in your life, those luxuries find a way of coming into your life at some point.

The helping family had never been greedy, had never stole a single thing, nor had they ever asked for more than what they were owed.

This positive behavior and chain of moral actions eventually led them to have everything they ever wanted in life.

Now they could live however they wanted, buy whatever they wanted, and most importantly, provide a stable future for their son.

What we often fail to realize is that every negative action we take, is negative towards us also.

For every thief that steals, he steals from himself, for every liar who lies, he lies to himself, and for every cruel person, he is only hurting himself. The law of compensation ensures that people get what they deserve, which is the result of their actions towards others and themselves.

You have to realize that no good deed goes unrewarded, no matter how big or small it is. People often think that the smallest of good deeds such as helping someone cross the road or picking up an empty carton of milk from the road and disposing of it are unimportant and hold no real value.

However, these small deeds can sum up to a lot of positive influences in your life. The goals you are looking to reach can be achieved and supplemented through the positive and noble actions you have taken in life.

And for those who have been victims of unjust actions, there is no need to hold resentment or anger towards the wrongdoer. It is healthy to let go of all the negative feelings and it will feel even better to forgive the wrongdoer.

Although it might seem like the most difficult thing to do, forgiveness brings the utmost level of satisfaction.

This is what defines supreme law of compensation. We are often unable to understand the experiences we go through until the point where we grasp this real truth.

Understanding how this law works will always bring you more tranquility because at the bottom of your heart, you are aware that you did no wrong.

And for all the good that you did, you can wait for all the positive reactions to come back, whether they are in the form of an appraisal at your work, a promotion, the perfect life partner, or a family that loves you unwaveringly.

The law of compensation has a way of balancing all the good and bad that we do. If we have our heart in the right place and approach everything that we do with no malice in us, not only will those goals be achieved, but we will get positive energy from our actions for the rest of our lives.

The law of compensation has to become engraved in our mind in order for us to follow it unwaveringly.

After you see the benefits it brings upon you, you will be ever thankful for adopting this law and using it in life.

Law of Non-Resistance

The law of non-resistance is the idea that helps you overcome obstacles. Non-resistance is a tool that can help you push through problems that can cause interruptions on the path to reaching your goals.

Basically it is about not resisting those deterrents. The power behind resistance comes when you resist something continuously. If you do not resist anything, then it will not have any power.

To fully understand the power of non-resistance, you have to understand the power of resistance.

To make things easier, here is a little example for you to understand how non-resistance can change your outlook on life.

Take a fear you may have, it can be anything. A random example of a particular fear is something like having a fear of water.

If you fear water, then you'll never realize how fun it is to swim and to float around under the sun at the pool or in the ocean.

Now everybody has different degrees of fear, but if you fear water to the point that you don't go in it or even take a boat ride, your fear is quite severe.

The fact that you resist water, gives more power to your fear. The more you resist going into water, the more afraid you will be of it. What happens is that you emit negative energy towards your fear, in this case, water. In turn, that negative energy festers and becomes stronger, hurting you and causing you more dread. The more you resist water, the more anxiety you will feel towards it.

Eventually, you will resist the water so much that you will create a problem which you may feel is too big to overcome.

Now, through this anxiety, there will be a part of you that will feel weak.

You will feel that you cannot overcome your problem, therefore, allowing yourself to be defeated by a fear and not achieving your full potential.

This is not to say that you will not reach your goals just because you don't go into water, but you will remain disempowered in an aspect of your life because of the power you allow the water to have over you.

Because you emit so much negative energy towards water, you hardly have any positive energy left to fight against your fear, letting yourself be swallowed by a limitation which can create a hindrance when trying to reach your goals in life.

What is important to understand is that the power of resistance is strong, but it is you and you alone that can control it. While resistance may be strong, the power of non-resistance is stronger and more powerful.

So how do you know that you're limiting yourself? Well, not all fears will be as prevalent as a fear of water. You could unconsciously avoid certain things you don't want to deal with and not even know it.

So how do you know when you are resisting something? You know when you are resisting something when you struggle with coming to terms with it.

Struggle happens when you are basically pushing against the tide, not going with the flow of the tide. If you have enough courage to notice this about yourself, you'll realize that it is quite easy to stop resisting and start working with the tide. Although that does not sound like it is easy, it actually is.

To overcome your fears is to overcome all obstacles on your path to success. You need to believe in yourself and your abilities, and then move forward to overcome your fears.

The first step to non-resistance is to acknowledge that you have a particular fear, whether it be fear of heights, water, fear of failure, fear of other people, etc. When you realize that there is something limiting you from reaching your full potential, it will be easier to counter that. Taking immediate action against your fears and hindrances will help you become more successful in your life.

Now, when you acknowledge your fear, you are giving into it, which can be a little overwhelming. To admit that you have a particular problem with something can be hard, but knowing the problem is the first step in how to overcome it.

Once you have acknowledged the problem, you work on fixing it, whichever way you think will help you the most. With this immediate reaction, you will start noticing a change in your life.

After acknowledging your fear, you will automatically start to emit positive energy to overcome your fear. And now you know, when you emit positive energy into the world, you gain positive energy back.

By pushing the negative energy away and by replacing it with positive energy, you are attracting positive energy towards yourself which will help you solve your problem and never face it again.

Although this is easy in theory, in reality it can be hard, but persistence and patience is key. If a problem is not solved immediately, give yourself some time, think of a new strategy or approach, or see how the problem can work for you instead of against you.

By just acknowledging that you can push past your obstacles is a powerful tool that you have inside you and that will help you achieve every success in life.

Another factor that you want to include in the law of non-resistance is the fact that there will be times you feel uncomfortable.

This is natural, because life at times can be uncomfortable, but the best thing about the discomfort is knowing that you can push through it. Your life has a certain flow to it.

That flow can be interrupted multiple times, and when it is interrupted, it is up to you to know what power and ability you posses to overcome it.

When you come upon a fear or an obstacle and try to run away from it or go around it, it will automatically push against your tide, interrupting your path to success.

This ideology of running away from your fears will cause you anguish and anxiety for as long as you run from your problems.

Believing in yourself and believing in the law of non-resistance will help you make hard choices that you have been avoiding.

A part of growing up is not only aging, but is about taking more responsibility on yourself. When you take more responsibility, you are held more accountable. The power that responsibility and accountability gives you is a power that cannot be taken away by anyone or anything. You control your choices and your future, and by resisting any of your responsibilities you are selling yourself short.

To realize your full potential, you need to give yourself a chance. Push open that door of fear and figure out a way to counter it. It may not be easy and it may not be fun, but when you understand the power you possess you'll never let anything get in your way.

You may have to change your plan, your lifestyle, your entire ideology, but never let something stop you from achieving a successful future and destiny, something you have complete and utmost control of.

Law of Forgiveness

The law of forgiveness is a law that can change the way you see your world. It is a law that appeals to your natural goodness and forces you to push negativity out of yourself and only emit positive energy.

To learn to forgive is a lesson that is timeless and can push you forward towards a successful future. Holding on to resentment and grudges distract you from focusing your positive energy towards your goal.

Forgiveness can be difficult at times, especially when someone has hurt you. Exonerating someone of a wrongdoing is more than just physically being civil with him or her, it is about mentally pushing past something that has caused you pain.

To emotionally let go of a bad situation is the only path to take when in a situation that makes you feel uncomfortable.

What it boils down to is pushing past negativity that others may push onto you, and using your positive energy to move forward.

So how does it work? Have you ever heard the expression "kill them with kindness"? The idea is to not allow anyone to let their negativity get to you.

Being kind all the time will help you focus on your positive outlook on life and will help you ignore negative energy that others may push onto you, at times on purpose and at other times accidentally.

And while being kind will help you push past other's negativity, that does not mean you should let people take advantage of you. If someone hurts you purposely, then it will of course have an emotional impact on you.

This is completely normal; you are a human being with feelings which can be intentionally or unintentionally hurt.

To allow you to live a healthy and happy life, you need to experience these emotions but then need to learn how to overcome these negative emotions which may fester into obstacles that will cause you interruptions on your road to a successful and happy life.

Essentially you need to learn how to forgive. So how do you do that?

So, first of all, you need to categorize those people who hurt you unintentionally and intentionally. Of course, in real life some people don't always necessarily see those who hurt them intentionally, but there are some tell tale signs.

In any case, pushing past negative comments made by either category is what your goal should be.

Now, we've all heard the expression "forgive and forget". It is a small piece of advice a parent, a teacher, or a role model may give you at some point in your life. To forgive and forget is good advice which encourages you to believe in your abilities and not let anyone bring you down.

Those who unintentionally hurt you should be forgiven and their comments or hurtful actions, forgotten. An honest mistake is just that, and should be forgiven.

The person who has hurt you unintentionally will apologize and will most probably right their wrong when you show some compassion and forgiveness towards them.

Your positive energy towards them will encourage them to push positive energy towards you and to even better themselves by understanding their wrongdoing.

The other category, the people who intentionally hurt you, they should be forgiven as well, but their negativity will always come back to haunt you if you continue to let them impact your life.

Forgiveness is, in all senses, a gift which should be cherished. Those who constantly hurt you neither appreciate the gift of forgiveness nor give it the value that it deserves.

Forgiveness is about respecting others, understanding that they make mistakes, and by allowing them the chance to start with a clean slate.

However, everybody does not understand the value or importance of forgiveness, and instead of giving them chances and being disappointed over and over again, you should forgive them and then keep your distance.

There are many people in the world who do not understand the power they possess through their energy, and therefore may not understand how much they can affect a person through an action or verbally.

The fact that you understand the power you possess and the fact that you can forgive someone is a power that no one can take away from you and that will allow you to reach your full potential in life and exceed it.

When you learn to forgive, you let go of the past. If there have been misfortunes or hurt in your past, the best thing to do is to let go of it.

Emotionally release the energy that still lingers on to those trials and tribulations and move forward with your full force and positive energy.

Your past is a guide that lets you know what was good for you and what was bad for you. It helps you realize who the people you need to keep in your life are, and those who are not important.

Your past should be left where it is and not dwelled upon. Help yourself by moving forward and letting go of those emotional impressions.

The most important lesson of the law of forgiveness is forgiving yourself for the past mistakes you have made.

By accepting that you are a human being who makes mistakes will help you forgive yourself.

Pushing forward with this realization will not only help you reach your goal for a successful and happy life, it will help you get there quicker. Your mistakes teach you how to be a better person, and as a good person, you should cut yourself some slack and move forward with your life with a clean slate.

Law of Sacrifice

The law of sacrifice is a law which allows you to understand that in order to gain something new you'll have to give something up.

Although this can sound daunting, it is not. It helps you realize the value of moving forward in life by letting go of past things.

The law of sacrifice is about valuing that which is important to you in your life at the time. It is about giving value to the things that deserve extra attention and by moving forward from things that may not be as important anymore.

It takes a certain amount of discipline when putting the law of sacrifice into practice. You have to let go of something in order to receive something new. It is like the concept of giving something to get something.

This is a hard law to practice and can be a little scary. Letting go of things that may have been of value to you once creates uncomfortable situations to you as you travel into new territory.

Many times people are resistant to let go of things that were once important to them because either they don't want to put any effort into sacrificing something or because they don't believe it will work. When you sacrifice something, you will not immediately see the benefits of it.

The importance about these universal laws is that they require discipline and patience. Nothing comes easy, and because you change your outlook on life by following the laws of the universe will not mean you will never have to work for what you want.

Appreciating your own power and the unison in which you and the universe can work in together is not only life changing but pushes you to better yourself and your life.

In order for the law of sacrifice to work you need to believe in yourself and the power of the universe.

When it comes to the law of sacrifice, you have to understand that this law does not mean sacrificing your health, loved ones, or your integrity.

In order to achieve your goals, you should not hurt yourself or someone else.

Success is never about pushing others down in order to get yourself up.

Again, all of these disclaimers have to do with truly understanding these universal laws and appreciating the powers that unite you with the universe to gain your goals.

The law of sacrifice can be a little confusing at times. It is difficult to know what to sacrifice and how to sacrifice it.

So in order for you to fully understand it, here are a few examples of what the law of sacrifice entails.

For instance, if you decide to get married, you are giving up the life of a single person and gaining a companion.

You sacrifice all things that came with being single to gain everything that comes with being married. Another example is when you need to buy something, such as a new car or a computer.

To gain one of these objects, you must sacrifice money. Letting go of the money will give you the opportunity to have a new car or a new laptop that can potentially help you achieve your goals. The same goes with weight loss.

Dieting will get you the body you want, but you'll have to either give up some food or exert energy when exercising.

Now both of these aspects, the thing you sacrifice and the thing you gain, have good points and bad points. But focusing on the good points is what matters most to reach your goals.

There are many distractions in life and misrepresentations. TV shows and movies romanticize success into a 30-minute show or 2 hour movie, showing success as a quick achievement.

If anyone has ever worked for what they wanted, then you'll know it's not as easy as sitting around and thinking about it. It's about doing. And just as hard work is about the actions you take, sacrifice is about the actual sacrifices you make in order to reach your goals.

One of the most important things to remember when practicing the law of sacrifice, and any of the other laws, is that misfortunes and hardships will occur in your life multiple times and all throughout your life.

Staying the course and giving yourself positive reinforcement is the way you can get through everything if you want it to. Many times people who do not gain what they want will blame the bad luck on fate, others, the world, etc. It is always easier to blame someone else or something else instead of yourself when hardship strikes.

It's true, all calamities are probably not your fault, but the fact is, if you find yourself in an uncomfortable position, it is up to you to get yourself out. It's just like the expression "when life gives you lemons, make lemonade!" Take responsibility for bad things that may happen to you in life will help you cope with them better.

The effort it takes to right a wrong uses a lot of your energy, therefore, when something does happen, it's easier to accept that it has happened and then to outline a plan on how to overcome the problem.

The willpower you possess is unstoppable when you want it to be, and it is important for you to realize that.

Every situation is what you make it, and if you are served some misfortune in life, you have the power to turn your situation around.

Law of Obedience

The law of obedience is a law that encompasses all the universal laws and expresses that by following each law with discipline will help you achieve the success you want to.

Following anything in life takes discipline and dedication; the laws of the universe are no different.

If you take shortcuts or don't follow universal laws as you should, you will probably not gain the positive goals you want to in life and it will take longer for you to reach the success you want. Just like any law of the land, the law of obedience should be a law that molds your lifestyle.

You would not necessarily run a red light or take something that isn't yours because it is illegal and disobeys the law of the land.

By the same token, you should not abuse or try to cut corners when trying to achieve success in life because you will be hurting yourself by not allowing yourself the full potential to shine.

While disobeying universal laws don't seem as bad as disobeying the law of the land, it is. When you suffer from disobeying universal law, you will see it within your own life.

So how do you know that you are disobeying universal law?

Well, first of all, you'll want to see in what aspect of your life you have any shortcomings. For instance, if you allow your fear of water from keeping you going on a Caribbean vacation, then you are disobeying the law of non-resistance.

Not giving into your fears will keep you from reaching your full potential, and therefore is allowing your fears to lead your life. In another example, if you feel that your life is not going as you want it to, you are probably disobeying the law of attraction.

Remember, positive energy attracts positive energy, and if you think you are doing enough, you might not be. Pushing yourself to be positive and to really want the things you want is key to obeying the law of attraction.

It is so important to know the laws of the universe to know whether or not you are obeying or disobeying them.

When you obey universal laws, you work in harmony with the earth and nature.

Natural energy interacts with natural energy, therefore, knowing what kind of energy to emit in certain situations is very important to make sure your life is happy, healthy, and successful.

The law of obedience not only stresses knowing the laws of the universe, it pushes you a step further and helps you realize why certain things may be happening in your life. If you disobey laws, then you won't have the results you want in life.

At times you may not be aware of the laws, and that is why knowledge of these laws is so important, especially if you want to improve your life.

Educating yourself will empower you and will show you a path to take to ensure a healthy and happy future.

Law of Success

The law of success is a law that stresses to all human beings that they are inherently intended to succeed. The way we have been made allows us unlimited powers to use at our disposal.

To properly use and harness these powers will ensure that we are successful in life, in all aspects like health, wealth, and character.

By understanding that you have been given a gift, you will automatically start to realize the power the laws of the universe hold, and how to use your power in harmony with the universe to ensure you are everything you can be and get everything you want.

When it comes to success, you have to understand that you are capable of everything and anything you believe in.

As humans, we have the same limitless capabilities as each other, but the reason we all live different lives and are at varying financial, health, and character degrees, is because we use our abilities and powers at different levels. When you understand the intelligence and the power you have within yourself, you'll want to learn how to hone that energy and benefit from it.

To believe in the universe and yourself is the first step to success. The forgotten laws of the universe are then a guide to help you follow a path that will ensure your unity with the earth and your success in life.

Understanding the pure power within yourself will help you achieve everything you want in life. And with time comes experience, and with experience you can right your wrongs as you learn more and understand the powers of the laws that can help you make a future for yourself.

Experiencing the laws of the universe solidify your understanding of just how much power is in this universe. When you follow the law of success, you'll know that it does not fail, ever, when used properly.

When you have the idea of succeeding in your head, you will. And as you move forward with your plan to succeed, there may be some hiccups on the way, but learning from your mistakes, planning, and dedication is what it takes.

All of these actions have to do with you directly, so understanding that you hold the key to your future is vital for the law of success to work.

The law of success is not only about succeeding, it is also about moving towards a bright future.

Moving forward from the past is the way to succeed in life, by not letting anything hold you back. If you do not move forward, you are not following the laws of the universe.

As you make progress moving forward, you can see how your life is shaping up. Taking note of what is working and what is not is important when it comes to planning for the rest of your life.

Learn from your mistakes or hindrances and keep trekking along to your success.

The Law of Success was originally a 1925 publication by a man named Napoleon Hill. The book composed of hundreds of interviews he had done for over two decades, with millionaires across America. The published work offered 16 original lessons (another one was added later) for a person to follow to ensure their life was as successful as these millionaire's lives. Each lesson offered people insight into how these men had become millionaires and acted like a guide for people to try and be successful.

Interestingly enough, a few of the tips have to do with the laws of the universe and the power within yourself.

The first tip Napoleon Hill talks about is the idea of working with like-minded people. He specifically warns new businessmen/women of others who may give off negative energy towards the potential business or other business partners which could cause a business to fail. When working with like-minded people, you are able to excel because of the positive energy. The next tip has to do with focus.

When you know exactly what you want you can use your best talents and abilities to help your business thrive.

Knowing what you want will not only help your business, it'll help all aspects of your life. Also pointer is self-confidence.

If you believe in yourself, then others will believe in you. If you don't believe in yourself, then no one will. You must practice the law of non-resistance to face your fears and push through any doubts or obstacles you may have.

Self-confidence comes to you when you no longer give fear any power and understand that you have all the power you need to do whatever you want to do. Ignorance is also a trigger for fear, so make sure you are knowledgeable in your endeavors as well.

Throughout his advice, Hill warns of veering off the path. This is the same as disobeying the laws that you need to follow for your successful life.

So make sure you are dedicated and completely invested in yourself and your success.

Most of all, being creative and dedicated is a main argument in Hill's book.

Being completely invested in your business pushes you to be positive towards it and emit positive energy. He stresses on enthusiasm for your endeavor. Going that extra mile to get what you want will only help you, never hurt you.

What is most interesting in Hill's publication is that most millionaires are in the position they are because of how they approached their endeavors.

Because they handled their project with focus, determination, positivity, and dedication, they were able to reach a height that they weren't even aware of. A business can be profitable if you want it to be profitable.

Yes the idea needs to be a good idea, but if you put in the time and effort that the business or project needs, then you will see results.

And interestingly enough, Hill does talk about failure to create profit, just like the law of sacrifice and the law of non-resistance. Hill tries to take the negative connotation of failure out and tries to help a new businessman or woman use their "failure" as either a way to learn how to proceed forward or a temporary glitch that will not set you back.

It can be helpful instead of hurtful, maybe pushing you to rethink certain decisions or trying to make you think of another option instead of the one you've chosen.

If intentions towards the business are good then there is no reason anything negative should happen to your business. Do not look at failure as failure, give it a positive spin and keep trucking forward towards your goal.

Failure is not defeat, it is just part of your plan's outline, steering you away and towards certain paths which will help you reach success.

The last point in Hill's book is to treat everybody as you would expect to be treated. To be successful, you need to give what you want to get. Known as the Golden Rule, this principle is the principle that you need to follow in order to make all the other ideologies work.

Hill says that if you do not follow this rule and hurt others as you progress on your path to success, you are in danger of getting back bad karma. Whether good or bad, the energy that you emit with other people will come back to you at some point in your life, so you should always focus on positive energy.

Following this law will ensure that you never have any negative feelings such as lying or greediness as you progress with your business.

The law of attraction comes into play when discussing energies being attracted to energies. If you are positive and stay positive, that energy will come to you continuously.

How to Work With the Law

So now that you know about all the forgotten laws of the universe, you need to know how to work with them. The way that the universal laws will work for you is if they are practiced properly and with your full dedication.

Having a clear focus of what you want in life and then using the laws to gain your success will be beneficial to you and your future.

Each law is interconnected and none can act alone. They are meant to be practiced together and become a lifestyle change. Each law holds its own power and you are the one who controls its supremacy in your life.

Now as the laws of the universe unfold in your life, you need to be prepared to handle them. One key factor when it comes to the forgotten laws is change.

Change is vital to having a successful life because change is about keeping an open mind and realizing that the universe moves forward with each day and that we as human beings must follow suit.

As we are connected to all energy, we need to understand the importance of moving forward in life.

As you move forward in life you learn more, experience more, and experiment more. With each experience and event in life you are growing, maturing, and learning.

Each of these aspects are important to your personal growth and to your character.

When you experience something and don't like the outcome of the incident, you have the option to change the outcome and to prevent the occurrence from hurting you or becoming an obstacle on your path to success.

Every day is a new day and every day is renewed with a clean slate. To understand the importance in that is vital to understanding the forgotten laws. Without growth you cannot move forward.

Have you heard the term, "forward thinker"? A forward thinker is a person who is not limited by any boundaries and can think beyond constraints. This person looks towards a bright future and thinks of things that have not been thought of ever before.

You do not need to be a forward thinker to necessarily understand the forgotten laws, but you should strive to be a forward thinker to benefit to the fullest extent from the universal laws. When you think with no constraints, you allow your full potential to shine, with no inhibitions.

You allow your life to move forward with positive thoughts and energy. You let go of the old thoughts that may be holding you back. Those old thoughts, while at one time were important, don't stay important forever, therefore you need to let them go in order to improve your life.

When you push your mind to think above and beyond of normal thought, you allow your natural intelligent self to flourish. You must guide your mind; don't let your mind guide you.

Think about that statement for a second. Do you guide your mind, or do you let your mind guide you? If you let your mind guide you, you may be losing out on your creative and intellectual thought.

By expanding your mind and not limiting yourself, you could be tapping into thoughts and abilities you never knew you had. Also, by guiding your mind, you can open y our mind up to things that you want to focus more on.

If you want more money, make your mind focus on more money. If you want to be healthier, push your mind to think more about health related thoughts. Push the boundaries and expand your horizons so you can gain everything you want and need.

Your thoughts may be idealistic, but you can turn those ideal thoughts into practical thought and something that can actually help you get to where you need to be.

Remember that your thoughts are who you are. They are so important that they define your character and your future, so spending time on what your priorities are and how you want your future to unfold is a wise decision. And with a thought you have a power.

The energy that is generated by your thought is so powerful that it can change the way you think, it can change the environment around you, and it can change your future. With this amount of energy and responsibility, you will need to practice discipline.

Discipline helps you narrow down the things that you want and helps you differentiate from things that are important to you for the moment and things that are important to you in the long run.

It is true, as we get older we have different wishes, and so it is important to not constantly want things that will only give you short term happiness or pleasure. With discipline, you can hone in on your wishes and you can carefully control the power of your mind.

The power of the mind is the most important tool you have and should not be manipulated. That is not to say that you cannot make mistakes, but you should obey the laws of the universe and properly to correct any wrongs. This is why the laws are in place, to help you completely focus on what you want and to get exactly what you want.

The power of the mind is so strong that it makes and breaks problems and solutions. When you say, "I have a problem", you have to understand that you don't actually have a problem, the problem is all in your mind.

Most problems are made within our minds and are not actually problems when we get down to it. We give events in our lives more power by the way we interpret them. To understand this idea is extremely vital for you to understand how you and the universe work together.

There are many things that influence the way you feel, think, and act, and many times these influential things are not natural, but are manmade.

Societal norms are boundaries that keep us contained in a bubble, not allowing anyone to be too different or to convey unique or "abnormal" ideology.

The connotation that comes with the word abnormal is negative, but it should not be. If something is abnormal it is not usual, not what the norm would be. It does not mean there is something wrong, it just means that something is unique.

However, if normal or abnormal thoughts and actions get you to your end goal, without disrupting the harmony between you and other living things, then it should be accepted.

Most of the time people are too insecure to think outside of the box and therefore limit the power of their mind. But it is important to know that through the power of your mind you can strengthen your thoughts and strengthen the path on which you want to reach our goals.

With your strong thoughts and powerful mind you have complete control of your inner self and the world you create.

You find validation in the things you think and the things you do because of your complete self belief and confidence in the path you choose to take to success.

By believing in yourself you cleanse your mind of any distractions and focus completely on the things you want. By concentrating on the things you want, you heighten each sense and hone them into focusing on your goals.

Even through focusing all your senses into one thought is part of creating a more full and enriching lifestyle.

Understanding everything about the universal laws will help you get to where you need to go, but there is a thin line between thinking at the surface level and real thinking. This is where many people have trouble.

They may think they are thinking about something, but their thoughts are just surface level ideas. Thinking beneath the surface has to do with understanding what you really want.

Tapping into the truth of your thoughts helps awaken powers in you which improve your understanding of what you want. It heightens your sense and makes you mind more sensitive to the things you want. When you think just on a surface, you are not tapping into what you want, you are only passing time.

These surface level thoughts are for everyday activities which we perform. They do not have to do with our character or our inner-most desires.

It is through deep thought that you can build yourself and your character by coming to the realization of what your desired truths are. What you truly want in life is control by your deep thoughts, and only through these thoughts can we push for what we want.

Your future is controlled by these thoughts and what you want your real destiny to be is determined by these thoughts.

For example, when you find yourself making a decision or taking an action with complete conviction, you know you are doing it because you have no doubts in your mind about it. Those are when your true feelings are conveyed through your mind and to your body. They determine your true nature and character. These natural and unadulterated ideas have to do with universal harmony. Acting as one with the universe to receive the things you want to in life will help you reach your success goals.

It is important to train your mind so you can have clear thoughts as to what your destiny should look like.

When you know what you want, everything should follow suit. Always strive for what you want and you will find that your mind, body and soul will also push towards your goals. Your body is a unit which can be controlled through your goals and it is up to you to push how much power you want to use.

As you continuously focus on a life that will encompass all the laws you have learned, you will notice how quickly your life will make a turn for the better.

23371828R00048

Made in the USA
San Bernardino, CA
16 August 2015